Barack, Race and the Media: Drawing my own Conclusions

by David G. Brown

Cover Design and Illustration by David G. Brown and Jeff Gaddy

Back cover photography credit Derek Rothchild

Barack, Race and the Media: Drawing my own Conclusions
ISBN# 978-0-9818674-0-3 0-9818674-0-5

The contents of this book originally appeared in the Los Angeles Sentinel newspaper 2003 thru 2010 with the exception of unpublished work.

Contents

This book is dedicated to
Cleveland Gillis
May 9, 1950 - April 22, 2006

Thank you for your Friendship.

Acknowledgements:

My parents **Frank** and **Doris Brown**, and my family. My son and awesome journalist **Damon Brown**.

The Los Angeles Sentinel newspaper: **Danny J. Bakewell, Sr.** Executive Publisher/CEO,
Danny J. Bakewell, Jr., President/Executive Editor, **Yussuf J. Simmonds**, Assistant Managing Editor,
Christine Brooks Martin, Production Manager, **Brenda Marsh Mitchell** and **Brandon J. Brooks**.

The Managing Editors who have inspired, encouraged and frustrated me:
James Bolden, Lela Ward Oliver, Kathy Williamson, Ken Miller and Danny J. Bakewell, Jr.

The Association of American Editorial Cartoonists: **Joel Pett** and **Tim Jackson**
Blackage of Comics: **Turtel Onli**.

Jeff Gaddy, Joyce O. Clarke, Marian Fifi Locke, Lawrence Fletcher, Bernadette Johnson
and the many other individuals who have inspired and encouraged me on this incredible journey called **LIFE**.

FOREWORD

My colleague David G. Brown

An award-winning artist, **David G. Brown** brings art to the world through the creation of cartoons. He is an educator and an illustrator, whose work as an art instructor for youth is displayed throughout the community with the publication of comic books distributed in libraries and his political cartoons in *the Los Angeles Sentinel*, a Black weekly newspaper.

The publication of his first collection of political cartoons *"Barack, Race and the Media: Drawing my own Conclusions"* is of historical significance because it largely focuses on the first African-American nominee of a major party running for **President of the United States**, Democratic Senator *Barack Obama*. Who now is on the threshold of becoming the first African American president of the most powerful nation on the earth!

These pages also include snapshots of celebrities, global events, and myriad political figures who captured the attention of the world and fell under the scrutinizing pen of David G. Brown. Some will make you laugh, some will bring back memories, but all will strike a responsive cord.

My association with David as a fellow colleague at the Sentinel newspaper is one of respect and admiration. He has taken both his art and this newspaper to new heights, winning awards that have drawn attention to the high caliber of talent in the Los Angeles creative community. I have been a sounding board for his cartoons and am an ardent fan of his work; so it is with great honor that I introduce the latest work of my friend and colleague David G. Brown to the literary world.

Yussuf J. Simmonds
Assistant Managing Editor
Los Angeles Sentinel 2008

Documenting one of the most significant times in our lives

David Glenn Brown is an established artist whose work in the early 90s highlighted the devastation following the 1992 Los Angeles Civil Unrest. Now it's history-making time. With his collection of drawings amassed over five years as political cartoonist for the *Los Angeles Sentinel newspaper*, David was passed the baton from *Clint Wilson, Sr.*, who spent 45 years in the artist chair.

David came to the Sentinel during my tenure as Managing Editor and his drawings quickly won applause and praise from both staff and readers. Just to confirm our opinion in David's first year with the *Los Angeles Sentinel*, he was awarded the *National Newspaper Publishers Association's (NNPA)* prestigious *Merit Award* for "*Best Editorial Cartoon*" *in 2004.*

In this satirical collection of cartoons, David has titled, *"Barack, Race & The Media: Drawing my own Conclusion,"* he highlights the historic presidential run of *Illinois Senator Barack Obama* and other significant events.

As someone familiar with David's work and his brand of double-entendre humorous drawings, I know this keepsake book will cause laughter, memories of high profile events, and water cooler chatter. At this time in history and at this moment in David's career he has set the bar higher for himself with this collection. This book is an influential literary work sure to be embroidered into the fabric of our African American history. I believe it will become a collector's item, documenting one of the most significant times in our lives and I encourage you not to miss out.

James Bolden

INTRODUCTION

Being an artist is all about conveying who you are through your art

I grew up in a small town in South Jersey and remember at a very young age my desire to create. Whether it was a drawing, writing or designing the latest and greatest new super hero. It was clear to me I would be involved in the arts.

In the more then twenty years since moving to Los Angeles, I have used my skills as an artist in the entertainment industry, advertising/media, non-profit and community sectors to help others convey their ideas and concepts. The highlight has been the opportunity to be the political cartoonist for the *Los Angeles Sentinel newspaper*, the largest Black newspaper in the West and designated as number one newspaper by the *National Newspaper Publishers Association (NNPA)*.

Several years ago I attended my first *Association of American Editorial Cartoonist* conference and was one of four artist of color out of a group of several hundred in attendance. Being one of only a few African American political cartoonists in the nation it is not only a privilege but also an obligation to address the myriad of issues affecting our world from an African American perspective.

Now after more then five years creating weekly political cartoons for the *Los Angeles Sentinel newspaper*, it is my pleasure to present *"Barack, Race and the Media: Drawing my own Conclusions"* my personal statement and observations of the most recent current events.

Enjoy!
David G. Brown

Barack Obama

Barack Obama made history as the first African American nominated for President of the United States by a major political party. Now he is on the verge of being elected the first African American President of the United States of America! It is a historical time for America not since the civil rights movement in the 1960's have African Americans been as excited and interested in the political process.

My first Obama cartoon in 2004.

Featured in *The Race for the 2008 Democratic Nomination Book of Editorial Cartoons*.

ALL-AMERICAN
PRESIDENTIAL FORUMS ON PBS
MODERATED BY TAVIS SMILEY

I HAVE A DREAM THAT MY FOUR CHILDREN WILL ONE DAY LIVE IN A NATION WHERE THEY WILL NOT BE JUDGED BY THE COLOR OF THEIR SKIN BUT BY THE CONTENT OF THEIR CHARACTER.

MARTIN LUTHER KING JR.
AUGUST 28, 1963

Obama'08

45 YEARS LATER, THE DREAM IS STILL ALIVE...

2008

DEMOCRATIC DEBATE 2008

WWW.DAVIDGBROWN.NET

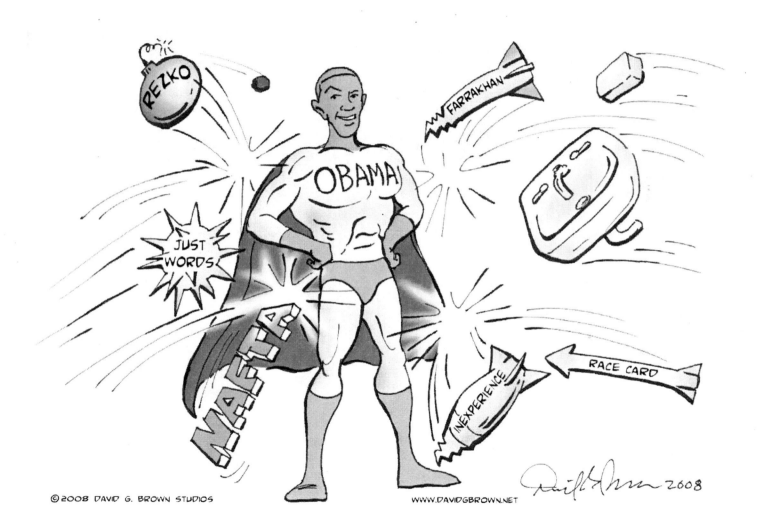

© 2008 DAVID G. BROWN STUDIOS

WWW.DAVIDGBROWN.NET

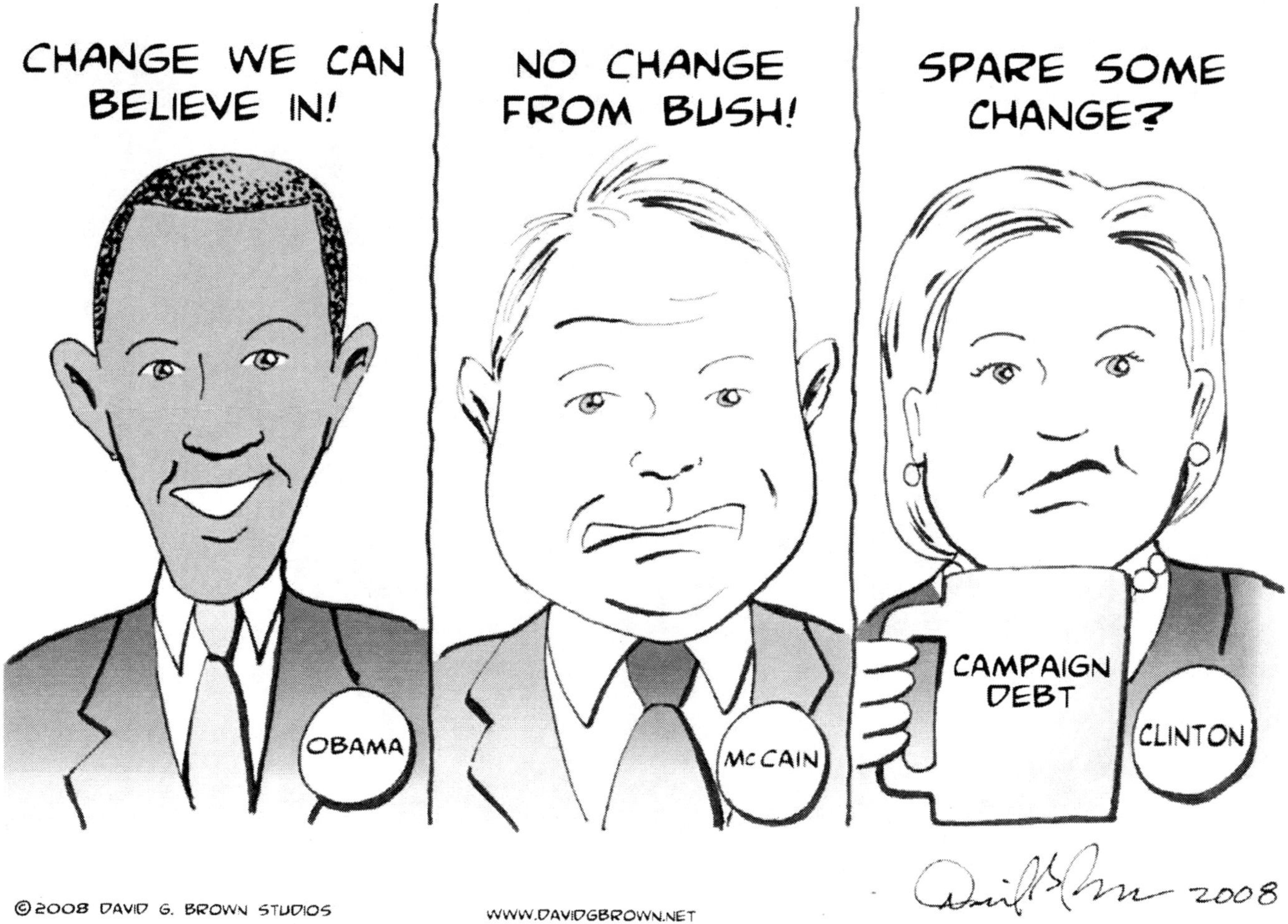

WWW.DAVIDGBROWN.NET

HOPE AND EXPERIENCE HOPELESS AND INEXPERIENCED

MISS VICE PREZ

© 2008 DAVID G. BROWN STUDIOS   WWW.DAVIDGBROWN.NET

THE 800 POUND GORILLA IN THE ROOM.

WWW.DAVIDGBROWN.NET

© 2008 DAVID G. BROWN STUDIOS   WWW.DAVIDGBROWN.NET

Award Winners

I have been honored to be awarded the prestigious *Merit Award for Best Editorial Cartoon* by the *National Newspaper Publishers Association (NNPA)*. I have won six of these awards since I have worked at the *Los Angeles Sentinel newspaper*.

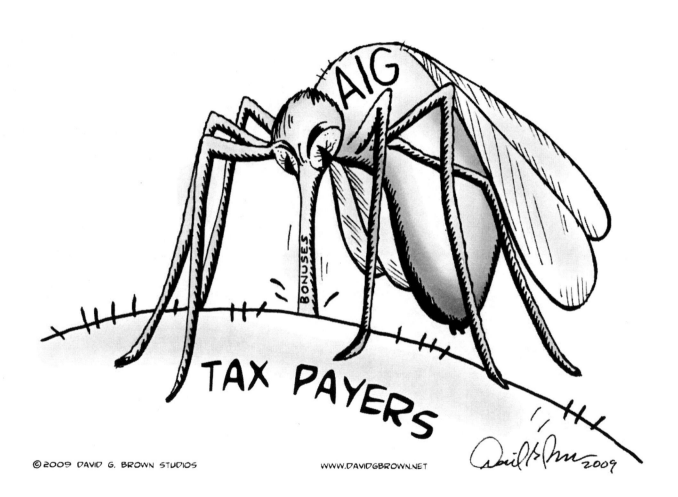

National Newspaper Publishers Association Foundation 2008 Merit Award

National Newspaper Publishers Association Foundation 2006 Merit Award

BALCO Arthritis Pain relief Cream*

BEFORE   AFTER

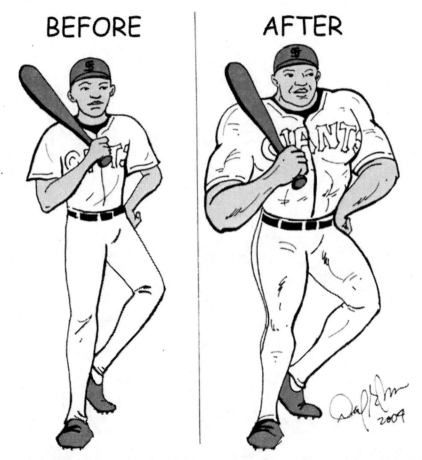

*Side effects may include increase muscle mass, strength,
mood swings, aggressive behavior, headaches, nausea and lying.

Celebrities

With a society obsessed with celebrity news, their public embarrassments, outbursts and missteps they are easy targets for jokes and criticism. At the same time there is sadness to their plight. From *Paris* to *O.J.* to *Tiger*, here are a few of my favorites celebrity cartoons.

Paris Hilton's legal woes.

Michael Richards using the "N" word.

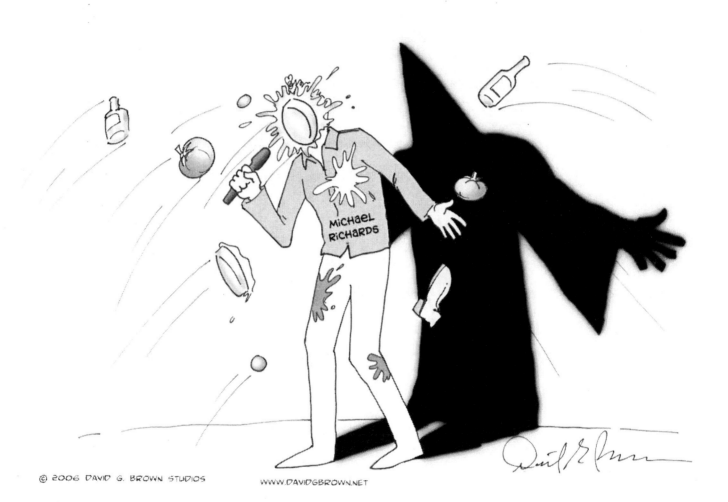

WWW.DAVIDGBROWN.NET

Robert Blake joins O.J. in search of the **REAL KILLERS**.

Bush Years

From *"Weapons of Mass Destruction"* to *"Mission Accomplished"* *George W. Bush* is considered by some to be the worst President in modern *U.S. history*. His failed policies, lies and poor judgment were some of the reasons I was inspired to become a political cartoonist.

THE CLEAN UP WOMAN

I received the most HATE mail for this cartoon.

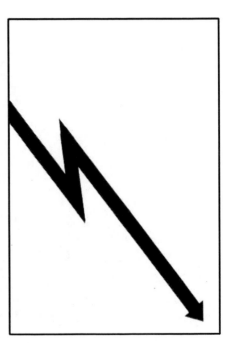

CAUSALITIES IN IRAQ   GAS PRICES   BUSH'S POPULARITY

IRAQ BENCHMARKS

SECURITY

ECONOMICS

CIVIL VIOLENCE

GOVERNANCE

REPORT ON IRAQ

THE SURGE

© 2007 DAVID G. BROWN STUDIOS   WWW.DAVIDGBROWN.NET

2007

FEMA

Federal Emergency Mis-Management Agency

2005

WELCOME BACK TO NEW ORLEANS...

WHERE WE TREAT YOU LIKE A (RODNEY) KING!

President Bush's report card
Terrorism F
Jobs F
Budget F
War in Iraq F
Civil rights F
Corporate Crime D-
Foreign affairs F
Diplomacy F
Arrogance A+
Teachers comments: Should be trained for another line of work.
2004

Remember Al Sharpton's run for President?

Brown vs. Board of Education

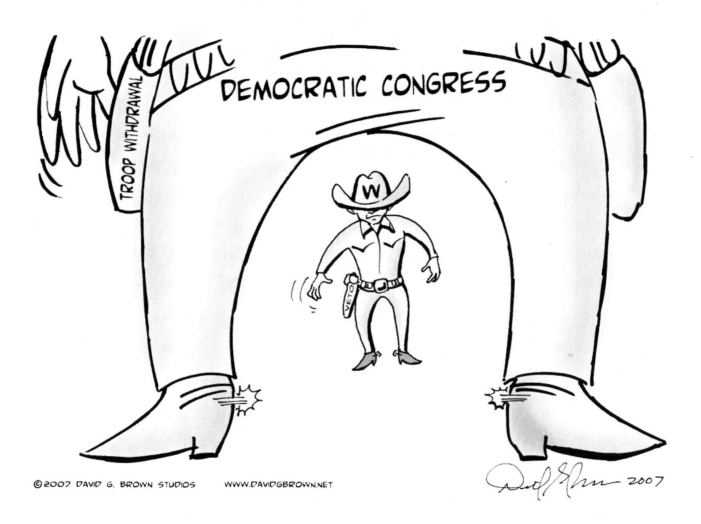

and other issues...

The *economy*, *foreclosures*, *police abuse*, *civil rights*, *security*, *gas prices*, these cartoons address some of the issues that have impacted our communities and nation in recent years.

One of the youth of America's biggest problems.

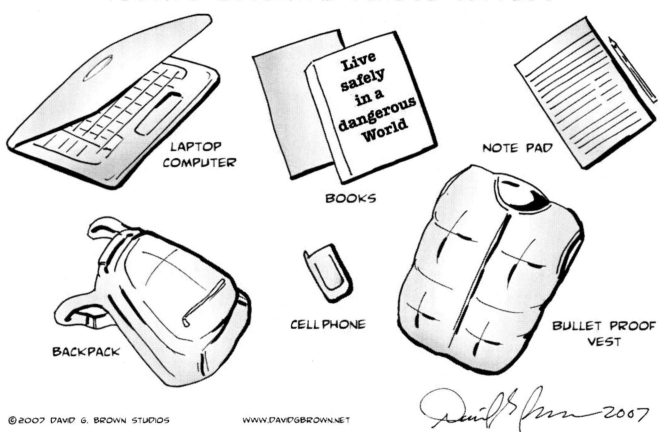

Los Angeles Catholic church payoff.

WWW.DAVIDGBROWN.NET

AIDs at 25
25 Million deaths
and counting...

LITTLE ROCK 9 50TH ANNIVERSARY

LITTLE ROCK CENTRAL HIGH SCHOOL

ONE OF AMERICAN'S MOST IMPORTANT CIVIL RIGHTS EVENTS.

2007

CAUTION

SWINE
FLU

WWW.DAVIDGBROWN.NET

© 2009 DAVID G. BROWN STUDIOS

© 2010 DAVID G. BROWN STUDIOS   WWW.DAVIDGBROWN.NET

10 years later...

O.J. is still looking
for the killers.

THE OLD BALL AND CHAIN

unpublished

These cartoons were trounced by other ideas, did not meet my editor's approval or for one reason or another never made it to print.

WWW.DAVIDGBROWN.NET © 2007 DAVID G. BROWN STUDIOS

...we will do what it takes...
the work of recovery is
moving forward.

George W. Bush
August 2005

...this town is better today than
it was yesterday.

George W. Bush
August 2007

This is the same SHIT we had last night!